D0394306

LIFE INSIDE THE
MILITARY
ACADEMY

AILEEN WEINTRAUB

HIGH
interest
books

Children's Press®

A Division of Scholastic Inc.

New York/Toronto/London/Auckland/Sydney

Mexico City/New Delhi/Hong Kong

Danbury, Connecticut

Book Design: Dan Hosek
Contributing Editor: M. B. Pitt

Special thanks to Kirk Schneider, David Radford, Jiordan DiOrio, and Jason Mattila

Photo Credits: Cover, pp. 31, 32, 35 © Joseph Sohm/ChromoSohm Inc./Corbis; p. 5
© NASA/Corbis; pp. 7, 23, 24, 26 © Bob Krist/Corbis; pp. 8, 11, 12, 16, 20 courtesy of
Defense Visual Information Center, March ARB, California; pp. 9, 37 © Corbis; p. 10
© Robert Maass/Corbis; p. 13 © Duomo/Corbis; p. 15 © Richard Hamilton Smith/Corbis;
pp. 19, 21 © Leif Skoogfors/Corbis; p. 28 © Karen Mason Blair/Corbis; pp. 29, 40
© Bettman/Corbis;

Library of Congress Cataloging-in-Publication Data

Weintraub, Aileen, 1973-
Life inside the Military Academy / Aileen Weintraub.
    p. cm. -- (Insider's look)
Includes index.
Summary: Explores the challenges and rewards of attending West Point
Military Academy in West Point, New York, where individuals are trained
to become officers in the United States Army.
ISBN 0-516-23921-X (lib. bdg) -- ISBN 0-516-24004-8 (pbk)

1. United States Military Academy--Juvenile literature. [1. United
States Military Academy. 2. Occupations.] I. Title. II. Series.
U410.P1 W45 2002
355'.0071'173--dc21

                                                          2002001904

CONTENTS

Introduction   4

1 A Rich Tradition   6

2 Getting In   14

3 Daily Grind   22

4 Diversions From Duty   30

5 Life Beyond the Barracks   36

New Words   42

For Further Reading   44

Resources   45

Index   47

About the Author   48

Introduction

General Patton. Presidents Grant and Eisenhower. Astronauts such as Buzz Aldrin, the second man to walk on the Moon. What single school can claim all these legends as alumni? They all graced the halls of West Point Military Academy. The faculty of West Point is fond of saying, "Much of the history we teach was made by people we taught." The purpose of West Point is "to provide the nation with leaders of character who serve the common defense." This means they prepare cadets for careers as officers in the U.S. Army. The academy strives to produce leaders.

These days, most young Americans want a college education. But some also want to serve their nation. For those young men and women, West Point might be a great fit. Admission to West Point is extremely competitive. Each year, the academy receives more than 11,000 applications. Yet they admit only 1,150 new cadets to their ranks. Along with a free education, West Point offers leadership development. Graduated cadets are guaranteed a well-paying job in the army. Most importantly, they become part of a tradition rich with history.

West Point is a challenging experience. But many cadets find that the rewards are equal to the hard effort.

All West Point graduates dream of going far in life. But, in 1969, Edwin "Buzz" Aldrin may have gone the farthest—all the way to the Moon!

CHAPTER ONE

A Rich Tradition

West Point Military Academy is located in the town of West Point, New York. West Point lies along the Hudson River. During the Revolutionary War (1775–1783), the town was a strategic military post. General George Washington appointed Thadeus Kosciuszko to design West Point's fortification in 1778. In 1779, Washington made his headquarters there.

During the Revolutionary War, colonists dragged a 150-ton iron chain from West Point across the Hudson River. Known as the Great Chain, this iron tool was built to help block British ships from traveling on the Hudson. Colonists would fire cannons at British boats as the boats struggled to free

themselves from the chain. Benedict Arnold, a former American war hero, tried to sell the plans for the chain's location to the British. This is how Arnold became one of America's most famous traitors. Luckily, the British never captured West Point.

TRAINING GROUND

After the war, officials of the new United States made a decision. They felt a school was needed to train men in the art and science of warfare. By providing this training, the United States wouldn't have to depend on foreign nations for military help. In 1802, President Thomas Jefferson established a military academy at West Point.

Colonel Sylvanus Thayer was the most famous West Point superintendent. He served proudly from 1817 to 1833. Thayer became known as "the father of the military academy." Thayer made civil engineering the basis of the curriculum. He also

ACADEMY FACTS

Many refer to West Point as the Long Gray Line. That's because of the color of the cadet's uniform is gray.

FAMOUS GRADUATES

Over the years, West Point has produced many officers who have helped shape U.S. history:

- Robert E. Lee—The general in chief of the Confederate armies during the Civil War
- Ulysses S. Grant—President of the United States from 1869 to 1877
- Douglas MacArthur—Supreme commander of the Allied Powers, 1945 to 1950; one of the most decorated soldiers in U.S. history
- George S. Patton Jr.—Commanding general of the U.S. army from 1942 to 1944
- Dwight Eisenhower—President of the United States from 1953–1961 ⟶
- H. Norman Schwarzkopf—Commander in chief of Operation Desert Storm in 1990

Not all of West Point's famous graduates made their mark on the battlefield:

- Edwin E. "Buzz" Aldrin—The Apollo 11 crewmember who was the second man to walk on the Moon
- Edwin White II—The first American to walk in space
- John G. Hayes—President of the Coca-Cola bottling company

CHAPTER TWO

Getting In

Qualifying for West Point is no easy task. Potential students must meet many requirements. They must be high school graduates between the ages of seventeen and twenty-three. They cannot be married. They cannot have any legal obligation to support children.

Each West Point hopeful must be nominated by an approved source. This usually means a member of the U.S. Congress or Senate. Don't worry! You don't have to know the congressperson before you apply. Your nomination is based solely on your academic record, athletic skills, and extracurricular activities. Still, the competition is fierce. In a letter to a senator, one nominee claimed

To go from a West Point hopeful to an actual cadet, you have to clear a lot of hurdles.

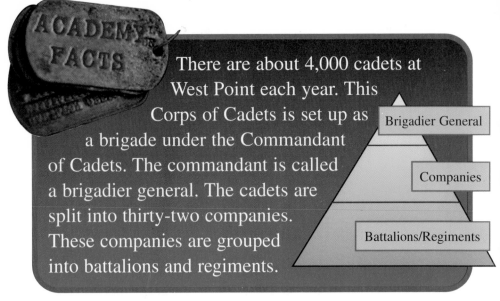

There are about 4,000 cadets at West Point each year. This Corps of Cadets is set up as a brigade under the Commandant of Cadets. The commandant is called a brigadier general. The cadets are split into thirty-two companies. These companies are grouped into battalions and regiments.

Brigadier General

Companies

Battalions/Regiments

to possess a strong ability with foreign languages. When the senator met that applicant, the two spoke entirely in French for the first five minutes of their meeting!

Applicants must complete a series of interviews and essays for West Point consideration. They also perform a physical aptitude test. This test includes a kneeling basketball throw, a long jump, and a shuttle run.

Hopefuls are expected to be near the top of their high school class. West Point applicants should have four years of both English and math. Math subjects must include algebra, geometry, trigonometry, and precalculus. Two years of both a foreign language and a lab science are required, along with one year of U.S. history. Excelling on the Scholastic Aptitude Test (SAT) or the ACT Assessment also increase your chance of being admitted. The best time to apply to West Point is junior year of high school.

Admission to the school is free. Room, board, and medical coverage are provided. Cadets also receive an annual salary of $7,200. This salary helps pay for uniforms, a computer, and other expenses. In return, cadets agree to serve five years of active army duty after graduation. They must also serve three years of reserve duty.

PLEBES

Freshmen are called plebes. Plebes comes from the word *plebian. Plebian* means peasant in the Greek language.

Most military training takes place during the summers. Plebes begin West Point with Cadet Basic Training during their first summer in the barracks. This six-week period is known as Beast. Beast is a grueling, stressful time.

During Beast, ceremonies, physical fitness, and proper appearance are drilled into cadets' heads over and over. Everyone gets a haircut!

There are only two styles: short and shorter. Male cadets get crew cuts. The hair of female cadets is cut to a short length. Plebes practice their marksmanship with rifles. They learn about military respect and courtesy. Beast demands that plebes work as a team. They must depend on each other to accomplish goals. Finally, plebes are given the jobs no one wants—such as carrying the laundry bags of upperclassmen!

YEARLINGS

Sophomores are called yearlings. They spend the summer before their second year at nearby Camp Buckner. Here, yearlings endure eight weeks of hard core military training. They learn squad and platoon leadership skills. They practice firing high-tech weapons. They also spend one week at Fort Knox in Kentucky. There, yearlings become familiar with armor and mechanized infantry equipment. Yearlings are given new leadership responsibilities, too. They begin to guide a few plebes in their company.

Cadets don't stop learning once the spring semester ends. But summer school for yearlings is a much different experience than for non-military sophomores.

COWS

Juniors are called "cows." This name comes from a time when junior cadets went on leave the summer after their yearling year. All the cadets would come back at once. This was referred to as the time "when the cows came home." The cadets must have looked like a herd of cattle heading back to a farm. During their third summer, cadets travel all over the world. They participate in specialty training programs. These include air assault training and mountain warfare.

FIRSTIES

Seniors are called firsties. This is because they are now first classmen. (Cows are also called second classmen. Yearlings are known as third classmen, and plebes, fourth classmen.) Firsties learn how to command large groups of cadets. They lead the corps during basic training and field training. They also prepare for platoon leadership responsibilities. Firsties get the most privileges at West Point.

ACADEMY FACTS

The year 2002 marks the 200-year anniversary of West Point's founding.

During their third summer, cadets jump into a new kind of training. The cows begin to practice what they would do during a battle.

CHAPTER THREE

Daily Grind

Cadets must follow an extremely rigid schedule, year-round. They begin their day at the crack of dawn. They must be at breakfast formation by 6:50 A.M. They start the first class of the day by 7:35. If you snooze, you lose. Missing a class often gets you into trouble. Cadets usually take between five and seven classes a semester. This averages out to two to three classes a day. Between classes, cadets receive some rare free time. If they're lucky, they may get to take a quick nap. Following classes, each cadet attends two hours of sports practice. Around 6:30 P.M., cadets eat dinner. They spend the rest of their evenings studying. Taps, the bugle call that signals lights out, plays at 11:30 P.M.

Students use the little spare time they have to study.

Cadets, such as this one, can't afford to take too many study breaks. They know instructors will be sending hard questions their way the next morning.

LEAVE TIME

All cadets have time off for Christmas and Thanksgiving. They also have spring and summer leave. Plebes start out with limited weekend passes. They may leave West Point for athletic, club, or extracurricular trips. Each year, the amount of weekend leave a cadet receives increases. Firsties begin with seven weekend passes. Cadets can earn more leave time by excelling in a certain area. Of course, they can also lose leave time if they break a rule.

THE CURRICULUM

The West Point curriculum combines physical sciences, engineering, humanities, and the social sciences. There are two parts to the curriculum. The first part consists of thirty-one core classes, which each cadet is required to take. The second part provides the opportunity to specialize in a single field of study. This course, or concentration, is similar to a major at a traditional college. There are twenty-four fields to choose from. Though not required to, most cadets choose a major.

Class size is kept small. There are between fourteen to eighteen students in each class.

Many classes are similar to those found at civilian, or non-military, colleges. Others, however, are unique to West Point. Cadets take classes in military art along with a course in leadership psychology.

If cadets break a code or a pledge, the punishment can be severe.

HONOR CODE

West Point prides itself on producing fine leaders. An important part of this process is the instilling of strong moral values in the cadets. Part of cadet training includes moral-ethical development. All cadets must live by an honor code. It states that "A cadet will not lie, cheat, steal, or tolerate those who do." This code is enforced without exception. The honor code's origin is based on the idea that a person's word is his or her bond.

Another code that cadets live by is "Duty, Honor, Country." West Point encourages cadets to be honest in all situations. Cadets are also expected to learn the seven army values. These values are: loyalty, duty, respect, selfless service, honor, integrity, and personal courage.

Each cadet is expected to memorize West Point's mission statement. The statement reads, "To educate, train, and inspire the Corps of Cadets so that each graduate is a commissioned leader of character committed to the values of Duty, Honor, Country; professional growth throughout a career as an officer in the United States Army; and a lifetime of selfless service to the nation."

TOUGH LOVE

Obedience to rules is a crucial part of cadet life. Some cadets find the strictness of the rules overwhelming. For instance, cadets are allowed to date each other. Yet they are forbidden to kiss or hug on school grounds. Unless the door is wide open, couples can't be alone in a room. They can't even hold hands.

Drugs, of course, are not tolerated. Cadets must undergo drug tests, sometimes monthly. They must wake up around 4:00 A.M. to be tested. These tests are administered throughout the four years.

FAMOUS DROPOUTS

- Mark Twain, the author of *The Adventures of Huckleberry Finn*
- Edgar Allen Poe, the writer of "The Fall of the House of Usher"
- Maynard James Keenan, the lead singer of the band Tool

Can I take your order, sir? If they slip up and make mistakes, West Point cadets know that they'll get an earful.

For some, the rules are too hard. These cadets find that military life is not suited for them. A student at West Point can drop out, although they must do so within the first two years. If they drop out within this time, they don't owe the army any service or pay.

CHAPTER FOUR

Diversions From Duty

After World War I, Superintendent Douglas MacArthur made an important change to the curriculum. He pushed for major changes in physical fitness. The new motto "Every Cadet an Athlete" became an important goal. Today, athletics are a crucial part of the West Point experience. There are intramural and competitive team programs. These include sports such as rugby, crew, and sailing. West Point cadets also compete both regionally and nationally with other Division I colleges. Intercollegiate teams include football, basketball, wrestling, hockey, and baseball.

All cadets must participate in a sports program each semester. This is to make sure

In the fall, cadets look forward to continuing their classic football rivalry with the Naval Academy.

When it comes to hard work and grit, West Point sports teams are stubborn as mules.

they keep up required standards of physical fitness. Athletics help cadets acquire, and keep, self-confidence, self-discipline, and team spirit. It also teaches them to think and act in stressful situations.

THE FACILITIES

Michie Stadium, located at West Point, holds over 40,000 people. It is home to the army football team. In addition, West Point houses a hockey rink and a basketball arena. The academy also has a golf course, a ski slope, and grounds for camping, hiking and hunting. There are swimming pools, wrestling, squash, racquetball, handball, and volleyball courts.

MASCOTS

Each of the thirty-two cadet companies has its own mascot. Mascots motivate the team and whip the crowd into a frenzy. These mascots include many things, from a fighting chicken to a man dressed in animal skins waving a battle axe. The official West Point mascot is the Black Knight. He pops up at all sporting events, rousing the crowd. The most famous animal mascots are the four army mules. They're known as Ranger, Trooper, Traveler, and Spartacus.

EXTRACURRICULAR ACTIVITIES

Almost every academic department at West Point has a club. Recreational activities include everything from martial arts to canoeing. There are student publications that cadets can become involved with. Cadets staff an FM radio station, WKDT. Cadets are encouraged to join choirs, the theater guild, or the glee club. The Cadet Fine Arts

Forum allows cadets to explore other interests. They get to try their hand in dance, photography, painting, and music.

PARADES

West Point cadets must participate in parades. There are two parade seasons. One happens around football season in the fall. The other begins close to graduation season in the spring. During football season, parades are held every Saturday morning before each game. Parades are also held for certain holidays or ceremonies. Often if a colonel or general is retiring, a parade will be held in that person's honor. Sometimes cadets act as saber-bearers in a wedding or participate in funeral ceremonies.

TRADITIONS

West Point is steeped in tradition. One formal tradition takes place during Christmas dinner. The corps sings "The Twelve Days of Christmas." Each section of the mess hall has a different part to sing. When it's a certain section's turn, one cadet will get up on the table. The rest of the cadets in the section lift up the table and sing.

Some cadets may sneak out and do things they're not supposed to do. These rule-breaking traditions tend to happen before a big game or during Term End Exam Week. They may be fun, but these amusements may come with a price! If the cadets are caught, they get punished for their antics.

Cadets wear many uniforms. Their most formal uniform is worn for parades and important dinners. This uniform is called Full Dress Gray over White.

CHAPTER FIVE

Life Beyond the Barracks

Cadets have a long road to graduation day. So when they finally throw their white hats in the air at Michie Stadium, they do so with pride. They've completed four challenging years. They're prepared for the next step in their military careers. After graduation, West Point cadets become commissioned officers in the U.S. Army.

Grads soon are told where they will be stationed. This refers to the locations and duties they will be assigned. Cadets have some choice in the matter. Some decide to stay in the United States. Others choose to go abroad.

How much choice a cadet has is based partly on class rank. Cadets with the highest

grades and honors get to pick first. This rank-based system continues until everyone has a slot. There are only so many slots for each location. After one location is filled, a cadet must choose an alternative location.

ON THE JOB

Army life introduces a world of new duties and opportunities. As officers, graduates often travel the globe. They get to work with fascinating people from many different backgrounds. They are given a lot of responsibility. Wherever they end up, officers become responsible for the training and welfare of many soldiers. They are responsible for making crucial, split-second decisions. They must act as role models for other soldiers. They are responsible for the maintenance of equipment, including weaponry, and they must keep up with technological advancements. This way they can use up-to-date equipment in times of war.

As time passes, officers prove and improve their abilities. As that happens, they advance in rank.

SPECIALIZING

West Point graduates must attend a branch officer basic course. The course teaches new skills, tactics, and expertise. During the first eight years of service, officers take additional training courses. Officers who continue their military careers beyond eight years can specialize further in a particular field. These fields include communications-electronics, engineering, and operations research.

The army has several branches of service. Each branch requires its own expertise. These branches include:

- Air defense artillery
- Armor
- Aviation
- Chemical
- Engineer
- Field artillery
- Infantry
- Medical service
- Military intelligence
- Military police
- Ordnance
- Quartermaster
- Signal
- Transportation

Projects such as the Panama Canal prove that West Point has turned out its share of gifted grads.

AFTER THE ARMY

Those officers who choose to stay in the army after their required time may go on to high leadership positions. Many take on government roles such as governor, congressperson, or ambassador. Others become educators and astronauts. Over one hundred former cadets have competed on U.S. Olympic teams. Engineers who have graduated the academy have been responsible for flood control projects around the world. They have helped construct the Panama Canal and build Disney World. Most West Point graduates feel that their time at the academy helped shape their life. They feel a real sense of accomplishment about their tenure at West Point. They realize that they can tackle any task, as long as they set their minds to it.

NEW WORDS

battalions groups of cadets that must work together

branches different divisions of the military

brigade a group of cadets made up of different units, such as infantry or armor

civil engineering the work of someone trained in the design and construction of things such as roads or bridges

companies a unit of cadets

expertise special knowledge of an area

NEW WORDS

infantry a branch of the army that is trained to fight on foot

intercollegiate competing with other colleges, usually in sports

intramural competing teams within one's own college

platoon a division of a company

regiments military units consisting of a number of battalions

FOR FURTHER READING

Efaw, Amy. *Battle Dress*. New York, NY: HarperCollins Children's Books, 2000.

Gartman, Gene. *Life in Army Basic Training*. Danbury, CT: Children's Press, 2000.

Hughes, Libby. *West Point*. Englewood Cliffs, NJ: Silver Burdett Press, 1992.

RESOURCES

WEB SITES

UNITED STATES MILITARY ACADEMY AT WEST POINT

www.USMA.edu

This is the official Web site for the USMA at West Point. It provides helpful links and answers to questions about applying for admission.

WEST POINT BICENTENNIAL WEB SITE

www.west-point.org/family/bicent/

This site offers an in-depth description of life at the academy.

RESOURCES

THE WEST POINT CLUBS HOMEPAGE

*www.usma.army.mil/uscc/dca/clubs/
    clubshome.html*

This site provides links to over one hundred different West Point-sponsored clubs. They include everything from the debate team to paintball and long-distance running teams.

INDEX

A
admission, 5, 17
Arnold, Benedict, 8
athletics, 30, 32

B
battalions, 16
branches, 39
brigade, 16

C
companies, 16, 33
cows, 20
curriculum, 8, 25, 30

D
drugs, 28

E
expertise, 39

F
firsties, 20, 25
Fort Knox, 18

H
honor code, 27
Hudson River, 6

I
infantry, 18, 39

J
Jefferson, Thomas, 8

K
Kosciuszko, Thadeus, 6

M
MacArthur, Douglas, 9, 30

INDEX

P
parade, 34
physical fitness, 17, 30, 32
platoon, 18, 20
plebes, 17–18, 20, 25

R
regiments, 16

S
salary, 17

T
taps, 22
Thayer, Sylvanus, 8
tradition, 5, 34–35

W
Washington, George, 6
women, 5, 11–12

Y
yearlings, 18, 20

ABOUT THE AUTHOR

Aileen Weintraub is a freelance author and editor living in the scenic Hudson Valley in upstate New York. She has published over 30 young adult and children's books, edits historical manuscripts and college textbooks, and works part time for a not-for-profit organization serving kids with special needs.